SHE WINS

Again!

More
Life Transforming
Inspiration to
Get Your
Mind Right and
Win in Life

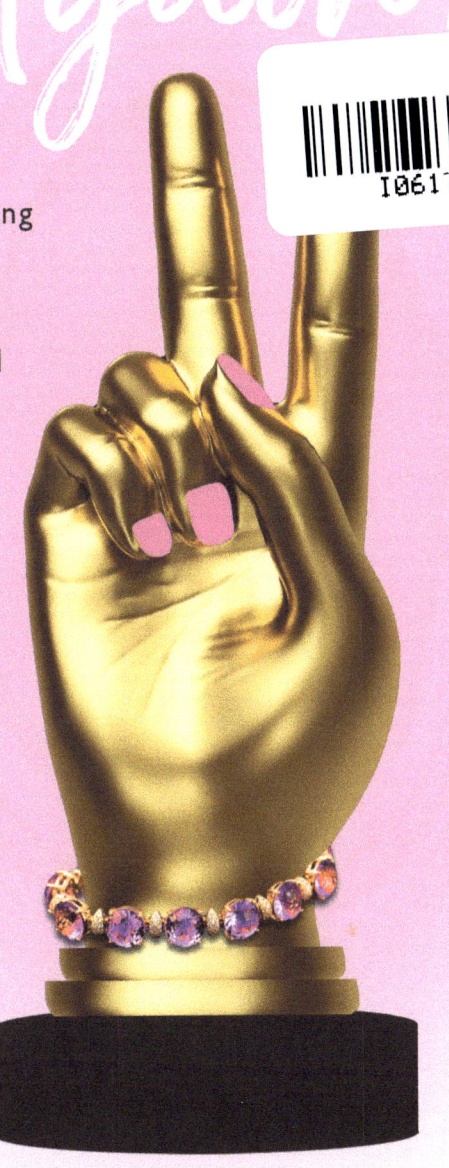

ANDROMEDA RAHEEM

ENDORSEMENTS

As a woman who is constantly growing and evolving, this book helps you not only visualize what a winning woman looks like, but also provides actionable items to help you along the journey.

— Shonda Brown White

Whether you win or lose, it's up to you! How powerful is this statement from Master Coach Andromeda? This statement checked me at the beginning. I had to think it through and determine if I was in the mindset to win. I knew from this statement that I was in for a ride with this book. Did I want to win or lose? I chose to win. The chapters set you up to take your surface thinking to deep meditation and inner working. The prompts that are asked set you up to choose to win. This book is next level winning, next level authenticity with oneself, next level self-care. Are you choosing to win? You better dive right in and set yourself up for a continuous winning streak!

— Coach Jas Stokes

Andromeda's ability to connect experience with actionable tips and relatable anecdotes makes becoming the CEO of your life doable. Taking control of your life looks like reading this book and doing the work!

— Kenisha B. McIntosh

DEDICATION

For Aneesah, thank you for showing me how to rise above adversity, make the best of all circumstances, smile on the toughest days, and love unconditionally. I miss you, godmother.

For Roger, thank you for being the best husband, teammate, and friend a winning woman could ask for. I love you deeply.

For my tribe, thank you for growing with me and never giving up on me. I appreciate you dearly.

FOREWORD

MY SISTER, ANDROMEDA, has taught me so much in my life. She has been an example to me of what it looks like to feel the fear and do it anyway. Her faith has inspired the restoration of my own in moments of unclarity. Her resilience has shown me that I can come back from any "loss" with a lesson in tow. Her courage to show up every day as herself has motivated me to do the same. Her journey empowers me because she doesn't pretend to stand on a pedestal. Her relatability shows that if she can do it, so can I and so can you!

My sister wins because she does the work necessary to grow. I have watched my sister manifest and create a life that she loves, not by magic or happenstance, but by doing the hard work. Over the years, she has turned the lens on herself and examined the difficult areas that most of us tend to stay away from. Her growth has been both inspiring and restorative.

Even in the midst of her growth, as she cultivated the beautiful woman she is today, she has been a servant to women. She wasn't hesitant about reaching out to the women around her and sharing the tokens of wisdom she's gained along her journey. Not unlike most women, she has had her fair share of scrapes and bruises. The beautiful thing about her is that she has used those very scrapes and bruises as a salve to help heal the women that she encounters.

Andromeda wins because she consistently creates spaces for women to show up as themselves, authentically. She is a champion of women, giving them permission to be the same. She gives selflessly because she acknowledges that another woman winning is not a threat but a boost.

As she continues to evolve, she will continue to serve. *She Wins Again* is Andromeda's assignment. It is a culmination of the lessons that she has learned on her journey of becoming a better woman. I pray that her words leave an imprint on your life, as they have done for mine countless times. I pray that they empower you to not only be motivated but also do the work.

Naimah Raheem

TABLE OF CONTENTS

INTRODUCTION

WHILE WRITING THIS book, I experienced loss that made me pause, illness that pushed back my publication deadline, and challenges that delayed my progress. The fact that you are holding this book in your hands is proof that you are capable of doing whatever you set your mind to do. The journey may take longer than you expect it to and you may have to change your plans along the way, but nothing is impossible with a winning mindset. Despite the unexpected curve balls life threw my way, I wrote this book and committed to finishing it in order to inspire you to never give up on yourself. It is my hope that reading this book will empower you to take control of your life, make the best of your circumstances, and continue to pursue your goals no matter what obstacles you face.

Since publishing *She Wins: The Ultimate Guide for Women to Gain a Winning Mindset and Lead a Winning Lifestyle*, a lot has happened. I've experienced life changes and gained transformational wisdom. Perhaps one of the most profound lessons I've learned is that life is a continuous journey of redefining what winning means to you. As you learn and grow, your definition of winning will change. And as your definition of winning changes, so will your goals, interests, and environment.

These days, my definition of winning is as follows:

Winning is to feel confident in your authentic self, be at peace with your decisions, walk fully in your purpose, rise above adversity, and achieve your own definition of happiness and success.

My perspective of what winning looks like has changed dramatically over the years. When I was insecure, unsure of my identity, and unaware of my power, I defined winning as receiving acceptance and validation from others. I set and achieved goals that I thought would help me prove my worth to others. I earned degrees, climbed the corporate ladder, spent a lot of time trying to grow my social media following, and strived to be featured on as many platforms as possible, all to prove that I was good enough. I am grateful for everything that I've accomplished over the years, regardless of what my motivation was because it proves that I am capable of achieving whatever goals I set, but I can honestly say that the wins I once valued don't feel the same now that I have a much higher sense of self-worth. I am no longer at the mercy of other people's compliments and criticisms because I am secure in who I am and confident in my own skin. I now celebrate wins every day, not just on the days when others acknowledge my work and efforts. I now set goals that fulfill me and my purpose as opposed to goals that are meant to gain attention and acceptance.

To redefine winning in a way that truly fulfills me, I had to do the inner work necessary to heal my past pain, increase my self-worth, get in alignment with my purpose, and trust myself to make decisions that are in my best interest. In this book, I share with you some of the most valuable lessons I've learned to be able to elevate in all areas of my life. I also share testimonies from amazing women that will inspire you to keep moving forward after loss, failure, and disappointment. This book is your guide and motivation to make choices that will lead you to live your happiest, healthiest, and most fulfilling life. Now, let's grow and win together!

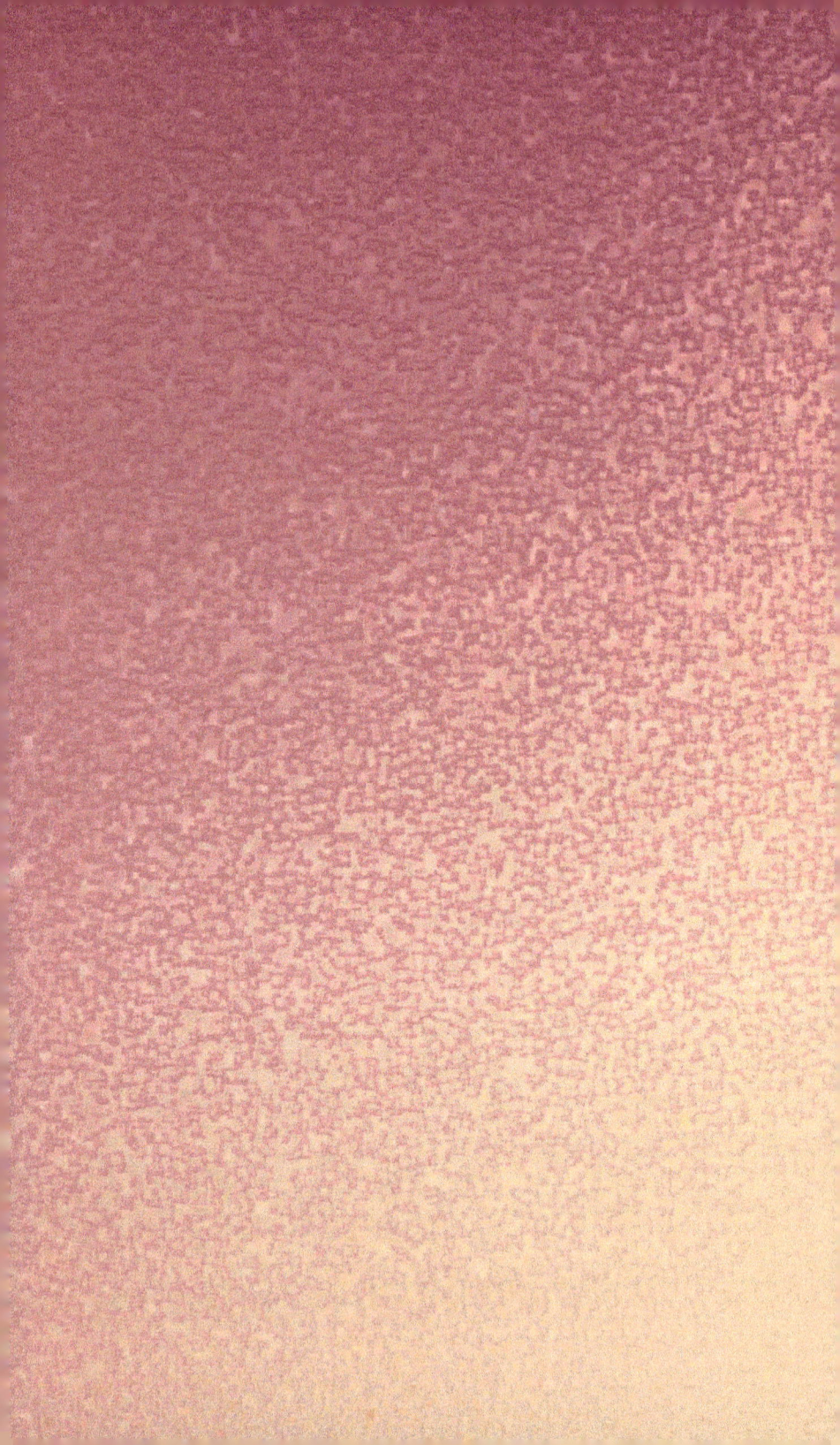

PART 1:

MINDSET & MOTIVATION

I:

SHE IS THE CEO OF HER LIFE

Winning women aren't just CEO's of businesses and they don't just call the shots in boardrooms. They also take life by the helm and take authority over themselves.

YOU HAVE THE power to choose what's best for you. Accepting this fundamental fact is how you promote yourself from being a victim of your circumstances to the CEO of your life. As CEO, you can implement policies that are in alignment with your highest good, hire people who see your value and vision, and fire anyone who attempts to disturb your peace and diminish your light. Once you step into your position as CEO, you will have the power to make decisions for the good of your mind, body, and spirit. You will act in your best interest and do what it takes to win.

I know very well what it's like to live as a victim. For quite some time, I was a victim of other people's attitudes and decisions. The way people treated me determined my mood, productivity, and confidence from day-to-day. I spent many days blaming others for my lack of joy and fulfillment. I was often miserable and constantly crippled by the actions of others. There were moments when I sabotaged my own success and dimmed my own light as a response to others' inability to see my worth and respect my presence. If any of this sounds familiar to you, trust me when I say that you can decide at any time to live a completely different life.

Once I had enough of living like a puppet on a string and allowing others to dictate how I moved, I appointed myself as CEO and started to take control of myself and my life. I accepted that whether I wanted to take accountability for the part I play in my life or not, my choices are ultimately what's shaping my reality. I became more aware of the power of my own thoughts and actions and accepted that no matter what happens to me, I can always choose how I react and respond. Then, I exercised my power as CEO by implementing new policies, and hiring and firing accordingly.

Whether you win or lose is up to you. It's up to you because regardless of what others do, your choices are the ones that matter most. You must remember that no matter what you encounter, you can always choose how you react. You always have the choice to react in a way that will be beneficial instead of detrimental to your success. In the face of adversity, you can choose to rise above your opposition.

When you're criticized and underestimated, you can choose to continue pursuing your goals. When you fail or make a mistake, you can choose not to carry shame. You can choose to forgive for the sake of your own peace and sanity. You can choose to get back up after you fall. You can choose to walk away from what no longer serves you. You can choose to love yourself more than the people and situations that come to discourage you.

Your life is what you make it. You have the ability to choose how you think, what you say, and what you do. You have the power to change your mind and your perspective. You have the power to shift negative energy to positive. You have the power to transform your life completely if you want to. You are never stuck in one way of thinking or being. Although there are many things in the world that you can't control, you can always control the thoughts you entertain, the words that come out of your mouth, and your reactions to other people. With each choice that you make, you are manifesting your reality. You are deciding whether you will create more peace and harmony or more chaos and dysfunction. Even when it feels like it, you are never powerless. You are actually more powerful than you think. Within you is the ability to manifest love and hate, healing and pain, abundance and deficiency. You have the power within you to bring light to the darkest spaces of your life by making healthier choices.

You will face challenges and obstacles just like everyone else in this world, but you are the one person in this world who can't afford to give up on you or give away your power.

You are the only person who has to wake up in your skin and walk in your shoes. You are the main person who has to deal with the consequences of your actions. So it is your daily responsibility to make choices that are in your best interest. If you want to win, you must choose to speak kindly to yourself even when no one else is complimenting you. You must choose to be your own cheerleader even when no one else is clapping for you. You must choose to unapologetically prioritize your health and wellness. You must choose to protect your energy and keep your thoughts positive. You must choose to ask for and accept help when you need it. You must choose to do the work necessary to create the life you want to live. It's up to you to take control of your life and save yourself. Blaming others for what you lack won't help you to heal or move you forward. No one else can give you peace, happiness, and success. You must choose to create it for yourself.

TAKE A MOMENT:

1. Write down the policies (beliefs, standards, and expectations) you currently live by. Eliminate the ones that are outdated and not in alignment with the woman you are working to become.
2. Determine what new policies you need to add and implement to ensure your peace, happiness, and success.
3. Take inventory of the people in your life. Who needs to be hired, fired, or promoted?

4. Determine the kind of culture you want to live in. It starts with you. What example will you set that will show the people around you how to treat you and one another?

I am the CEO of my life. I am owning my power and making decisions that are in my best interest. I am unapologetically honoring my needs and creating the life that I want. I am taking full responsibility for my peace, happiness, and success.

NOTES

II:

SHE IS IN CHARGE OF HER HAPPINESS

Winning women don't sit around waiting for someone to come along and make them happy, they take ownership of how they feel and choose to be happy now.

I WILL NEVER forget the day that I decided to take charge of my own happiness. I was driving home from another day of mundane work, feeling dissatisfied with how my life was going. Much like I did on most days, I started going down the list of things that weren't going right in my life. As the thoughts were going through my mind, I had a revelation that brought tears to my eyes. It suddenly became so clear to me that I was *choosing* to be unhappy. Of all the things I listed, there wasn't one thing that I didn't have the power to change. I could change my job. I could stop hanging out with people who didn't appreciate me. I could quit my own toxic habits that were causing me unnecessary stress and illness. My life could be completely different if I wanted it to be. I could create my own happiness if I was brave enough to change and willing to do the work. Armed with this new revelation, I wiped away my tears and made a commitment to take charge of my own happiness from that day forward.

There is only one person in this world who can truly make you happy, and that person is you. If you are looking for your family, friends, children, significant other, employer, social media followers, or anyone else in your life to make you happy, stop now. That is an unreasonable expectation of others and an unfair amount of pressure to put on your relationships. No one can love you enough, compliment you enough, give you enough attention, or spend enough money on you to make you happy if happiness is something you haven't found within yourself. The search for happiness doesn't begin with the acquisition of people or things. Just look around at the celebrities who have gained fame and amassed riches but still express discontentment with life and can't manage to maintain healthy relationships. Contrary to what many have been influenced to believe, more popularity and money doesn't lead to more happiness because happiness is an inside job. Happiness is something you define and create for yourself.

The reason why many people find themselves feeling dissatisfied with their lives is because they are chasing someone else's definition of happiness. They spend their lives following someone else's blueprint for success without ever stopping to define success for themselves. They think that acquiring more money and material things will bring them more happiness, but the joy they feel after increasing their income and making new purchases is often fleeting and hardly ever enough to keep them satisfied. Soon after, they find themselves back on the search for something or someone that will give them long-term happiness. Most people never find true happiness because they search for it in all the wrong places.

The secret to being happy is within you. Being happy is a choice. Finding true happiness begins with making the choice to define what happiness means for yourself. Then it's making the choice to live out your own definition of happiness even when others don't understand your decisions. Choosing to be happy is not letting the thoughts and opinions of others determine how happy you are. It's not solely depending on money, relationships, opportunities, or popularity to make you happy. It's making the choice to find out what truly makes you happy and taking the necessary steps to align with that. It's a choice to change the things that you are unhappy with. Your happiness is your responsibility and completely up to you. You don't need to wait for some special time, thing, or person to be happy. You can choose to be happy whenever you are ready. Happiness is not something you need to find, it's something you *choose to be*.

TAKE A MOMENT:

1. Define what happiness means to you.
2. Write down anything you are currently unhappy with.
3. Reflect on and write down the choices you can make to change what's making you unhappy.
4. Think about the moments when you felt most happy and what you were doing in those moments.
5. Make a plan to do more of what makes you happy.

I am keeping my thoughts, words, and actions positive. I am focusing on what's going right in my life and maintaining an attitude of gratitude. I am counting my blessings and embracing my unique journey.
I am choosing to be happy.

NOTES

III:

SHE ACCEPTS WHAT SHE CAN'T CHANGE

A winning woman doesn't try to change people into who she wants them to be, she accepts who people show themselves to be and responds accordingly.

YOU CAN LOVE them, try to help them, and set a good example for them, but don't think for a second that you can change them. This applies to anyone you can think of, family, friends, lovers, co-workers, etc. You can encourage them, try to influence their decisions, and attempt to guide them in the right direction, but you can't change who they are or make their choices for them. Understanding this is essential if you want to win. In fact, coming to this understanding is what helped me stop blaming myself for things that were out of my control, remove myself from relationships that weren't serving my best interest, and shift my energy to more productive projects. Realizing that being biologically related to someone is not an excuse to stay in toxic relationships nor a license for people to mistreat me, helped me create healthy boundaries and remove myself from relationships that were more harmful than helpful to my mental, emotional, physical, and even spiritual health. It also freed up space in my life for me to experience more healthy and wholesome relationships.

The truth is that people don't change until they are ready to change. When you think about how easy it would be for someone to come along and change you, that should really put things into perspective. How easy would it be for someone to change your beliefs and values? How easy would it be for someone to change your personality and way of doing things? How easy would it be for someone to erase your painful memories? Based on our own personal experiences, most of us believe that we know what's best for our lives and we don't make it easy for others to change our minds.

Once I accepted that not everyone wanted me to save them, I learned how to step back and give people space to live their own lives and make their own mistakes. Stepping back from someone you love because they continuously make poor decisions and completely disregard your feelings can be difficult. Accepting that you can't change the toxic traits of someone you care about isn't always the easiest pill to swallow. Having to grieve the loss of someone who is still living because their presence in your life has proven to be more harmful than helpful can be heartbreaking. I've had to do all of the above in different seasons of my life, and it was painful every time. However, making those difficult choices not only gave me more peace, they also created space for my healthy relationships to improve. By letting go of what I couldn't control, I stopped feeling guilty for others' choices and helped my loved ones to take more accountability for their own lives.

If someone is determined to continue being toxic and refuses to stop stinking up your life with their toxic behaviors, at what point do you decide to protect yourself? Is it worth it to lose a relationship that's weighing you down if it means that you'll gain peace of mind and improve your emotional health? Loving yourself more than your subscription to other people's issues is not selfish. No relationship is worth sacrificing your mental, physical, and emotional well-being for because everything attached to you is impacted by what you think and how you feel. To win, you must be wise enough to get up from the table when what's being served is destroying your health and deterring you from reaching your goals. It doesn't mean that you stop caring about people, it just means that you stop enabling dysfunctional behavior and start holding others accountable for their own actions. In the long run, accountability is best for everybody.

You are only responsible for your actions. The only person that you can change and control is yourself. You can't change how other people choose to behave, but you can decide what you want out of life, what you are willing to tolerate, and what you will or won't compromise on. The better you know yourself and what you need to be happy, the easier it will be for you to determine where and how other people should fit into your life. The more you get in tune with yourself and your highest good, the more you will attract relationships that serve you and disconnect from those that drain you.

Successful relationships start with meeting people where they are and giving them the space to be honest about who they are. From there, you can decide what, if anything, will be gained from the relationship and how much time and energy you want to put into it. Relationships are transactional, but you don't always get back what you deposit into them. That's why it's important to know who you're investing in and what you expect them to add to your life. It's also important to know what value you bring to the table so that you can be mindful of the kind of people you invite to sit with you. You can't buy love and you can't make people be who you want them to be. What you can do is know your worth, accept who people show you they are, and decide to settle for nothing less than what you deserve.

TAKE A MOMENT:

1. Take inventory of your relationships.
2. Is there anyone in your life who you're making an effort to help change for the better? If so, are they receptive to your efforts?
3. If they are not receptive to your efforts, what do you need to accept about them and change about *your* actions to gain more peace of mind?

I am accepting that I am not for everybody and not everyone is meant for me. I am in healthy relationships with people who value what I bring to the table. I am showing others how I want to be treated by what I choose to accept. I am surrounded by people who love, respect, and appreciate me.

NOTES

IV:

SHE GROWS GRACEFULLY

Winning women don't force, fight, and chase,
they flow and win with class and grace.

ONE THING THAT you can always count on in life is change. It's going to occur whether you want it to or not. There was a time when I tried to avoid change as much as possible because what was familiar felt safer and easier. I prayed for growth, but didn't want to go through the changes necessary to elevate. I wanted to transform from caterpillar to butterfly without experiencing the dark and lonely cocoon stage. However, after living long enough to realize that it is impossible to experience growth without change, I came to accept that getting uncomfortable and moving into unfamiliar territory is a part of the process of leveling up. I learned how to grow gracefully by embracing change instead of resisting it.

Elevation can't happen without separation. Just think about that for a minute. Separation has been the catalyst for your growth all of your life. You had to separate from your mother's womb to be born. You had to separate from your diaper and pacifier to learn how to be self-sufficient and self-soothe. You had to separate from your parents to start your first day of school. Each time you move to the next level of your life, you are required to leave familiar things behind. You have to lose some things along your journey to gain greater experience and opportunities. Once you fully embrace the fact that nothing can remain the same and grow, you will have a greater appreciation for when seasonal relationships and positions end.

One of the most difficult parts about growth is the distance that it sometimes creates between you and people you thought you would grow old with. When you don't recognize that the separation you're seeing is a result of the growth you're experiencing, it can feel like you're losing instead of winning. It is important to understand that you don't belong to anyone and no one belongs to you. We are all being pushed towards our purpose and destiny, and sometimes that means that our lives will move us in opposite directions. It's also important to understand that not all relationships are meant to last forever. Some are just meant to teach you something about yourself and prepare you for your next level. Coming to the end of a relationship isn't always a sign that you've done something wrong. On the contrary, it might actually mean that you're doing a lot of things right. When someone is removed from your life, it doesn't always mean that they're a bad person. It may just mean that they are done serving their purpose in your life.

Growing with grace means surrendering to your highest good no matter what that looks like. It's trusting the process and flowing instead of forcing. It's getting out of the way and allowing what's meant to be to be. You can't stop change from happening, but you can make the process more difficult by trying to force things to stay the same. You can actually sabotage your own success by trying to hang on to people and places you need to let go of to grow.

While growth is great, it has the potential to bring out the worst in people because it's uncomfortable. It often gets the darkest right before the next breakthrough, which can be frightening if you don't understand what's happening. If you're not mindful, fear can cause you to run from growth and sabotage your success or make desperate decisions in an effort to remain in control. Being aware of this is how you can best prepare yourself to grow. Instead of running from the discomfort and resisting the darkness, you will embrace it because you know that a better version of you is about to emerge. You can tell that you're in a season of growth when you start feeling pushed to move out of your comfort zone. The growth process shakes up your life and moves you from familiar to unknown. You may not like how it feels in the moment, but grow with grace because once the discomfort passes, you'll find yourself in a much better position and realize that it was totally worth it.

TAKE A MOMENT:

1. What changes are you currently experiencing?
2. How are you handling these changes?
3. Are you attempting to hold on to anything that you need to release to make room for better and greater?
4. Embrace the growth process by not focusing on what you're losing, but what you can potentially gain. What good can come from the changes that are happening in your life?

I am embracing change and moving with grace. I am flowing freely and living faithfully. I am at peace with what comes and what goes. I am doing my part to live my best life and trusting that everything that happens is for my highest good.

NOTES

V:

SHE COMMUNICATES EFFECTIVELY

Winning women don't just speak to be heard, they speak to get results.

WOULDN'T IT BE great if people knew what you needed without you ever having to utter a word? When I was younger, I really thought that I could get away with expressing myself with the looks on my face and my body language. Unsure of how to articulate how I was feeling verbally and afraid of being vulnerable and rejected, I made it difficult for others to understand me and give me what I needed. Being constantly misunderstood made me not want to be around people. I resented others for not being able to read my mind and respond to my unspoken requests for affection and support. Eventually, I grew tired of watching others speak up and get what they wanted while I was silent and miserable. So, I learned how to communicate the right way.

Learning how to effectively communicate is life-changing. One of the most powerful things about communication is the clarity it brings. A lot of questions in your head can be answered by opening up your mouth. There is no reason to go through life confused about how people feel about you or whether or not you are in a relationship that has a future. There is no reason why others should have to question what you want in a relationship and how they make you feel. Communication is the key to healthy relationships. It's how relationships grow stronger and last longer.

You may have heard the sayings, "you have not because you ask not," and, "closed mouths don't get fed." God gave humans the ability to communicate for a reason. Never take the power of communication for granted. I learned the importance of this shortly after I graduated from college and got my first entry-level accounting position. Young and ambitious, I worked hard with the intention of being quickly promoted up the corporate ladder. Working hard by my definition was coming to work and doing my job to the best of my ability. As an introvert who was socially awkward, I didn't network or fraternize with my co-workers. I'd sit at my cubicle with my headphones on and complete the work that was assigned to me. I knew that I did good work because I was told as much by my supervisors. However, whenever opportunities for higher-level positions became available, I was always passed over.

At first, I made assumptions about why that might be and got upset thinking about the reasons I came up with. Then, I decided to put on my big girl pants and schedule a meeting with my boss to get clarity on why I wasn't being promoted. What she told me completely shifted my perspective and taught me a very valuable life lesson. In short, she said that I did my job well, but I seemed unhappy being at work. By walking through the office with headphones on and isolating myself in my cubicle, the perception was that I didn't want to deal with people. If that was true, it didn't make me a good candidate for upper-level positions that required more human interaction. By the end of that meeting, I had all of the information I needed to get what I wanted. Being promoted from that point forward became effortless for me.

The people who rise highest and go farthest aren't always the smartest or the most talented. They're often the people who have mastered the art of communication. They know how to ask the right questions and get the most favorable responses. They know how to speak in a way that makes other people listen. They know how to listen as well. The purpose of communication is not just to be heard or get a point across, it's to get your desired result. That's why speaking out of anger hardly ever works. Words can come out of your mouth, but they're pointless if the person you're directing them at doesn't receive them. Before you speak, ask yourself what you aim to gain from the conversation. Let whatever your goal is determine your tone and delivery. You'll find that doors will open more easily and your relationships will run more smoothly once you become intentional about communicating effectively.

TAKE A MOMENT:

1. Think of a time when you didn't communicate effectively.
2. What could you have done differently to get the result you desired?
3. How will you communicate better moving forward?

I am expressing myself effectively and getting more of what I want and need from the people around me. I am having more positive conversations and getting more favorable results. I am happy in my relationships and elevating in my career.

NOTES

VI:

SHE IS PRESENT

Winning women don't dwell on the past or worry about the future, they fully embrace the present and make the best of the current situation.

BEING PRESENT WAS something I unconsciously knew how to do in my younger years. All the way up through my mid-twenties, I lived fully in each moment without worrying about what was going to happen in the next. I don't remember dwelling on the past or trying to predict the future. I didn't overthink my every move or calculate every risk. I just lived for each day and trusted that everything would always turn out okay. And despite finding myself in some really wild and crazy situations at times, I survived with a lifetime of memories that I wouldn't change for anything.

Once I reached my mid-twenties and started getting "serious" about life, I stopped being present because I became more focused on my future. I was so busy making plans for what I wanted potential days to look like that I was constantly missing out on the moments I had in front of me. I couldn't even fully celebrate my achievements because I was always thinking about the next thing I needed to check off of my to-do list. As I got older, I realized that life is too short to be missing out on any moments, so I started to value my time more. By my early thirties, I decided to find a healthy balance between being present and planning for the future.

Many of us go through life thinking that we always have more time. More time to make healthier lifestyle choices. More time to spend with people we care about. More time to make amends with people we love. More time to find ourselves, be ourselves, and experience true fulfillment. We make all these plans and do everything others tell us to do to be successful, but we sooner or later realize that nothing is guaranteed in life. The employment isn't guaranteed. The weather isn't guaranteed. The relationship isn't guaranteed. The future isn't guaranteed.

In 2020, the world as we knew it instantly changed. Something happened that no one expected or predicted. The Covid-19 virus showed up and interrupted everyone's plans. It canceled events. It changed human interaction. It stole jobs. It cut millions of lives short. If being present is something that you find yourself taking for granted, looking at how quickly things changed in 2020 should really put things into perspective. The only guaranteed moment you have is the one you're living right now. This moment is currently the most important moment of your life because the past can't be changed and the future is unknown. It's what you do in this moment that matters most because it will ultimately shape your future and your legacy.

I found a healthy balance between living in the present and planning for the future by embracing the fact that what I do today will manifest my tomorrow. I create plans according to the visions and goals I have for my life, but I don't worry or stress when things occur that interrupt or change my plans. I embrace each moment as it comes with the intention of learning all of life's lessons and receiving all of life's blessings. Whenever I run into obstacles and challenges, I say to myself, "You're driving the car, but God designed the road." When I run into a roadblock, I just assume that I'm being redirected to something better. I don't try to predict my future based on my current experiences because I know that storms come and go, tables eventually turn, and miracles can happen. I go through life with the belief that giving my best to every moment is the best way to predict that my future will be promising.

Whenever you encounter experiences that make you want to abandon the present to dwell on the past or worry about the future, keep in mind that you have managed to survive all of your toughest days so far. You are still here despite everything you've been through. You have overcome things you thought you couldn't come back from. You survived the past and it doesn't have to define your future if you make better choices in the present. You can't go back and you can't fast forward. The present is what matters most and is all you have for certain. Appreciate where you are and what you have now. Make the most of every moment and live life to the fullest. That's how you'll end up looking back with more gratitude than regrets. That's how you can guarantee that you'll always give and receive one hundred percent.

TAKE A MOMENT:

1. When you find yourself dwelling on the past or worrying about the future, bring yourself back to the present.
2. Observe the sights, sounds, and smells around you and how they all make you feel. Engage in the positive things happening around you.
3. Embrace the present by doing something today that you may not be able to do tomorrow.
4. Express gratitude for where you are right now.

I am grateful for the life I get to live today. I am making the best of where I currently am and what I currently have. I am available for present opportunities and experiences. I am giving one hundred percent to every moment and living every day to the fullest.

NOTES

VII:

SHE IS PATIENT

Winning women don't rush the process, they prepare for what they pray for and trust that they will always arrive at the perfect time.

BEING PRESENT IS so much easier to do once you start practicing patience. Being patient is something I learned to do once I accepted that being impatient was causing me a lot of unnecessary frustration and aggravation. Wanting things to be exactly how I wanted them to be when I wanted them to be caused me to be constantly stressed and anxious. Doing things sooner than I was mentally, emotionally, and financially ready to do cost me years of cleaning up mistakes I didn't have to make.

Patience really is a virtue. Having it is a sign that you not only have self-control, but most importantly faith. Have you ever thought about how long it takes for things that are truly meaningful and worthwhile to grow before you can actually see them? Most seeds take two weeks or longer to sprout after planting them in the soil. A baby typically takes nine months to grow in the womb before it comes into the world. It can take three years for a new business to see profits. Having patience means that you will put in the work consistently and trust that in due time you will see results. Being patient helps you to avoid making decisions out of desperation and prevents you from prematurely destroying something fruitful just because you can't see it manifesting yet.

The best things in life aren't created overnight. The most worthwhile relationships are worth waiting for. Be patient with yourself. Be patient with your journey. As women, time is often our biggest stumbling block. So many of us get tripped up when another birthday rolls around and we can't check off whatever goals we told ourselves should be reached by that age. Be married, have a baby, own a home, and be settled in my career by the age of thirty were the goals I set. I'm thirty-six now and I'm married, but I don't have any children yet, don't own a home anymore, and I quit my career as an accountant to pursue my purpose. I basically started my life over at twenty-nine years old when I quit my job, sold my house, moved to a new city, and started my own business, so nothing looks the way I expected it to when I was younger. I know that many women my age have checked off all the things on my list already, but I don't concern myself with that. I stay focused on my own journey and the lessons I'm learning along the way.

My husband and I were together for ten years before we got married. We knew that we were young and had a lot to learn about ourselves and each other before we made such a huge decision. Not everyone understood what we were waiting for, but we did. We got married when it was right for us and as a result, we're going on nine years of happy marriage. When I look at how strong our relationship is now, I'm glad that we were patient and didn't jump into marriage before we were ready to. I think if we had, we wouldn't be together today.

I published my first book in 2017 and never imagined that it would take me four years to write the next one. However, I am grateful that I waited and didn't rush to put something out just for the sake of being able to say that I wrote two books. Because I waited, I have so much more valuable content to share. I am confident that my words will have a much greater impact now because I am much wiser now.

What I've learned is that no one cares how long it takes for you to arrive, they just admire that you made it. Today, people around the world still marvel at the ceiling in the Sistine Chapel, which took Michelangelo four years to paint. When you think of women like Oprah, Beyonce, Michelle Obama, and Viola Davis, do you calculate in your mind how long it took them to achieve what they have, or are you simply inspired by their success? It's really not about how long it takes you to get to where you're trying to go, it's about the life you live and the choices you make along the way. Instead of seeing delays as denial or a reason to give up, look at them as extra time to prepare for the things you're praying for. Life is a journey. Be patient and embrace every moment. You'll get where you want to go and arrive where you're meant to be if you just keep going.

TAKE A MOMENT:

1. When you feel yourself getting impatient, pause and take a few deep breaths in through your nose and out through your mouth.

2. When you feel frustrated because you want something to happen quicker than it can at the moment, think about previous instances when delays worked out for the best.

3. Instead of allowing impatience to consume you, do your best to make the best of your current circumstances. Examples: Sing in traffic, call a loved one while standing in a long line, count your current blessings while waiting for new prayers to be answered.

I am making the most of my time and making the best of delays that are out of my control. I am sowing good seeds and patiently waiting for my harvest to grow. I am doing the best that I can and trusting in God's plans.

NOTES

VIII:

SHE DOESN'T COMPARE HERSELF TO OTHERS

A winning woman doesn't compare herself to others. She runs her own race and keeps her eyes focused on her own lane.

IN MY FIRST book, *She Wins: The Ultimate Guide for Women to Gain a Winning Mindset and Lead a Winning Lifestyle*, I touched on the topic of comparison and why it should be avoided. However, because I continue to meet with and coach women who struggle with comparing themselves to others and the consequences that come with it, I thought it was worth touching on again to remind you just how unreasonable comparison is and how detrimental it can be.

Comparing yourself to someone else is never a good idea and it's always going to be unfair. I stopped comparing myself to other women once I realized just how unique my life and journey is. When I was born, where I grew up, the family I was raised in, the schools I attended, the lessons I learned, the experiences I had, and the people I interacted with all shaped the woman I am today. While other women may have experiences similar to mine, no one in this world has experienced life in my skin and through my eyes. No one else has experienced the same trauma, struggles, losses, illnesses, grief, and challenges that I have in the exact same context and on the exact same timeline. Knowing this, I can't justify any reason to look at another woman's life and compare where we are on our journeys. We are two different people, walking two separate paths. There is just no way to fairly compare myself to anyone. And the same goes for you.

Comparison is not only the thief of joy, it's also a catalyst for jealousy and envy. You can make yourself feel worthless and ungrateful when you start to measure what you have in comparison to those who seem to have more. It doesn't benefit you to put yourself in that position because there's no way that you can be bitter and win bigger. You can't be ungrateful for what you have and do the best with what you have. You can't minimize your worth and fully show up to get what you deserve. You can't have an envious heart and be genuinely open to learning from and collaborating with people who have gained more knowledge and achieved more success. If you are intimidated by the success of other women, you will miss out on opportunities to elevate beyond your current position. Comparison ignites insecurities that impede progress. Steer clear of it.

The only person you should be comparing yourself to is the woman you were yesterday. That's the only comparison that will make a real difference because as you get better, your life gets better. Life is not about being like someone else or keeping up with others. It's about finding yourself, becoming your best self, and creating your own path. Not to mention, your real life will never be able to measure up to the highlight reels of someone else's life. You never really know what people are going through. Some of us are really good at masking our pain and showing only what we want to be seen. Comparing yourself to others is a set-up for failure.

If you see someone achieving something that you want to achieve, be inspired but don't compare. Life is not a race and you are not in competition with anyone. See the accomplishments of others as proof that it can be done, not some false confirmation that you are falling behind or moving too slow. The best way to win your own race is to run your own race. Stay in your own lane and focus on your own progress. The better you get, the bigger you'll win. Compare yourself to no one and be your only competition.

TAKE A MOMENT.

1.   When do you find yourself comparing yourself to others?

52

2. How does it make you feel when you compare yourself to others?
3. What do you love most about being you?
4. What can you do to feel better about yourself and your life?

I love the woman I am today and the woman I am becoming. I am confident in my skin and proud of my accomplishments. I am using the gifts and talents I was given to the best of my ability. I am embracing my authentic self and comparing myself to no one. I am only in competition with myself and getting better every day.

NOTES

IX:

SHE LOVES HERSELF MORE

Winning women don't put themselves last on their to-do list in an effort to appear humble, they put themselves first to show that they know their worth.

YOU NEED YOU to win. If you really want to win in life, you have to love yourself more than all the stuff that tries to rob you of your health, peace, joy, confidence, and ambition. You need to love yourself more than the pressure society puts on you to be someone else because being confident in your authentic self is how you attract the people and opportunities that are meant for you. You need to love yourself more than the people who discourage and underestimate you because you can't make your dreams a reality if you don't believe in yourself. You need to love yourself more than your unhealthy habits because everything you consume has an impact on how you think and move.

Throughout my life, I have experienced tons of trials and challenges that tested my faith, character, and determination. I have set goals and faced numerous obstacles on the path to achieving them. I have been discouraged by the actions of others. I have felt like giving up. However, I always keep going no matter what because I know that if I quit, I am choosing to lose. I know that if I give up, I am choosing to settle and will have to accept the consequences that come with it. I can live with doing my best and having things not work out exactly the way I expect them to, but I can't live with giving up too early and not knowing what giving my best could have afforded me. No matter what I face, I always choose to love myself and my future more than whatever is threatening to defeat me at the moment.

One of the best gifts you can give yourself is the commitment to find out what life looks like when you intentionally put forth your best effort in all areas. You may have some setbacks with your health, finances, relationships, etc, but you can always choose to make a comeback. You can choose to love yourself and your life more than the things that knock you down and get you off track. At any time, you can choose to take back control of your life and rewrite the way your story ends. It's not over yet. You still have time to get it right.

Self-love is the best love because the more you love yourself, the more love you will have to give to others. The better you feel about yourself and your life choices, the more confident and valuable you will be in your relationships. Loving yourself more may sound selfish, but it's really the most powerful thing you can do for your family and anyone else who depends on you. You can't give what you don't have. You can't help others if you're sick. It makes it much more difficult to encourage others when you're feeling discouraged. By loving yourself more, you not only set the standards for how others should treat you, but you also teach people how to treat you.

When you love yourself it shows. It shows up on your skin and in your conversations. Your perspective on life changes and so does your energy. You become a more pleasant person to be around and start to attract love and positivity more effortlessly. You have less stress because you are more proactive with your health and overall wellness. When you love yourself, you feel better, look better, and do better. You are a better steward of your responsibilities and have so much more to give.

If you are like so many women who constantly find themselves last on their to-do list, stop feeling guilty for putting yourself first and start loving yourself more. No one gets a badge of honor for burning themselves out, and you're not the only one who loses when you neglect yourself. Love yourself more and everyone attached to you will thank you. It's truly a win-win.

TAKE A MOMENT:

1. Evaluate your current daily routine. If your days aren't beginning with at least 15 minutes of self-care, create a plan to change that.
2. If you struggle with feeling guilty about putting yourself first, imagine what would happen to the people who depend on you if your mind and body stopped functioning properly.
3. Think about how much more you could do and give to others if you had more energy and confidence in yourself.

I am taking good care of myself. I am giving myself the love I want to receive from others. I deserve to feel healthy in my mind, body, and spirit. I am keeping my cup full so that I can continue to pour into my loved ones and fulfill my purpose.

NOTES

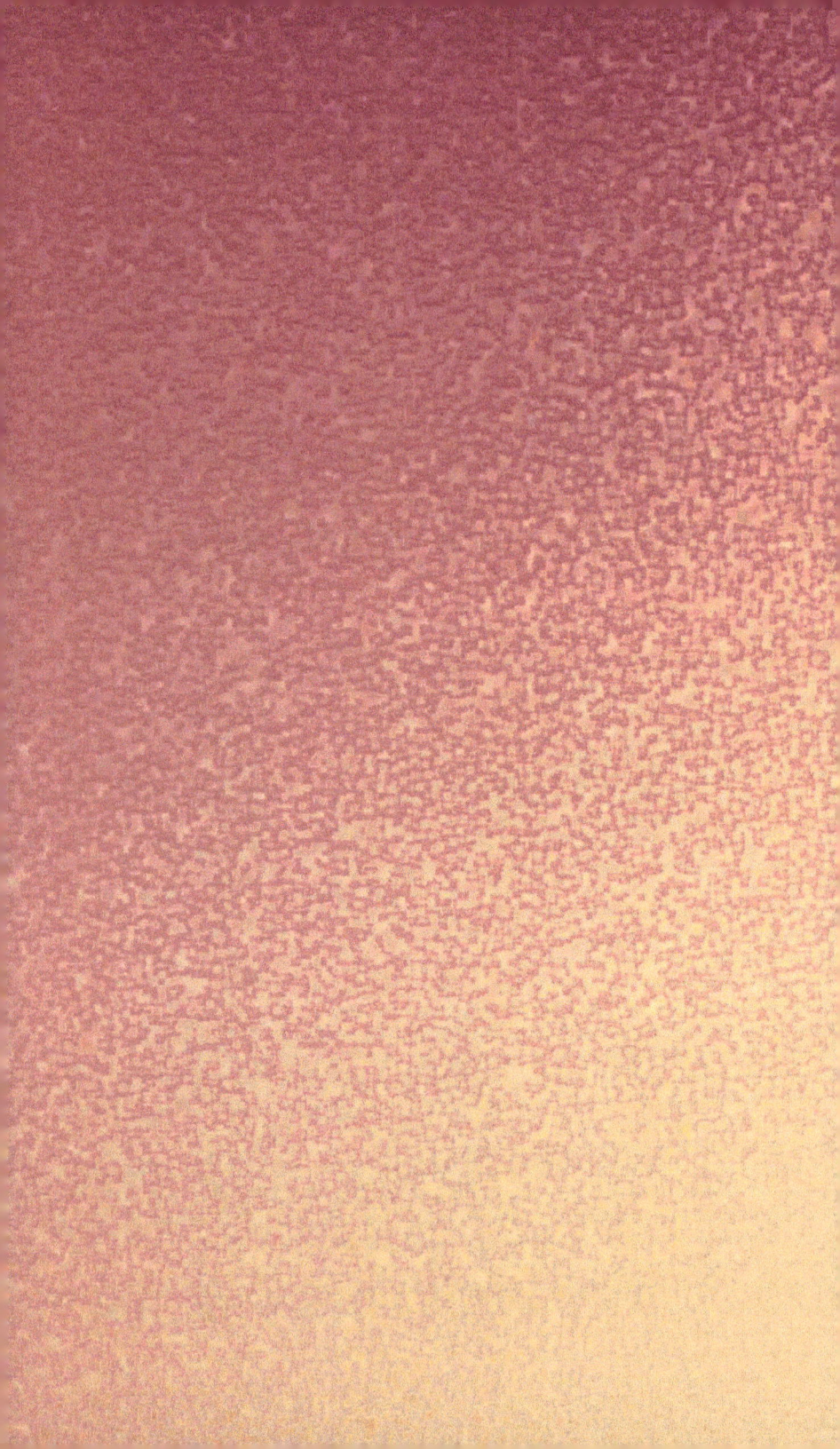

PART 2:

WORK & WIN

I:

SHE BOUNCES BACK

She wins because she won't stay down forever. She will always come back stronger, wiser, and better.

AS LONG AS you're living, pursuing goals, and interacting with other people, you run the risk of failing, being betrayed, and getting your feelings hurt. Life won't always be pretty and not everyone you encounter will be thoughtful and honest. You may experience situations that break your heart and crush your spirit. You may have moments when you feel like love and loyalty are myths. You may have times when you want to close the door to new connections and quit chasing your dreams. You may even start building up walls around your heart to save yourself from future heartache and disappointment. However, if you really want to win, you have to remain open and present. You have to be resilient.

Resilience is a trait that highly successful people have in common. At some point in our lives, we all experience loss, heartbreak, betrayal, and failure. I've experienced plenty of these instances myself. However, those who tap into their ability to bounce back from those experiences without losing zest for life and enthusiasm for reaching their goals are the ones who reach heights that most others don't. Maintaining a positive mindset and ambitious spirit throughout all of life's challenges is not always the easiest thing to do, but it's something you must be determined to do if you want to get the most out of life and rise to your fullest potential.

Imagine that you are a basketball and the air inside of you represents all the things you were given to succeed in life. Included are love, trust, hope, faith, and ambition. When you were a new basketball, you were completely full and perfectly shaped so that you would have the ability to bounce really high. Then, you began to play in the game of life and had moments when you landed in rough terrain. Inevitably, you were punctured by heartbreak, loss, betrayal, and failure and some of your air (love, trust, hope, faith, ambition) started to seep out. Depending on how quickly you patched up your holes and replaced the air that you lost, you are either still bouncing high or slowly deflating.

Life can get hard and sometimes you will get hurt, but you can't let tough situations change you into someone who can't win. If you stop giving love, you'll stop receiving it. If you stop trusting people and making new connections, you won't grow beyond your current level. If you stop having faith and ambition, you won't try new things and discover new opportunities. So if you've lost some air (love, trust, hope, faith, ambition) on your journey and it's affecting your ability to bounce as high as you want to, it's time to heal and refill. It's time to make peace with the things that hurt you and replace negative experiences with positive ones. It's time to renew your mind and gain a renewed perspective on life. It's time to take what you've learned to stop being bitter and start getting better. It's time to make your way back to the person you were created to be and become the woman you were destined to be. It's time to bounce back so that you can soar higher.

TAKE A MOMENT:

Fill in the blanks.

1. I lost _____.
2. I lost it when _____.
3. After I lost it, it changed how I _____.
4. I need it back because _____.
5. I can get it back by _____.

I am a survivor and an overcomer. I am stronger and smarter than the things that try to hold me back from living my best life. I am resilient and determined to win. I am rising above challenges and bouncing back from setbacks. I am unstoppable and undefeated.

NOTES

II:

SHE MAKES PEACE WITH HER PAST

She wins because she doesn't let the past define her present or have dominion over her future.

I HAVE ALWAYS been pretty resilient, or so I thought. I have been through traumatic, heartbreaking, and spirit crushing situations, but have always managed to pull myself up and push myself forward. I learned at an early age how to smile through my pain and hide my struggles. I thought that I was resilient because I knew how to carry my baggage without letting others see how heavy it was. I didn't understand that being resilient was much less about appearing strong and much more about recovering quickly. I was like that slowly deflating basketball that I mentioned in the previous chapter. On the outside, I appeared fine because no one could see the holes that I was covering up. Externally, it looked like I was whole and secure, but internally, I was slowly losing air and finding it more difficult to disguise my pain. It became clear to me that if I wanted to keep going, I was going to have to stop hiding my holes and start healing them. Rising to my next level required me to decrease the weight of the baggage I was carrying.

You can't outrun the pain from your past. Eventually, the baggage becomes too heavy to drag and starts to hold you back. If you never release it, you eventually become stuck in it, replaying the same sad stories, repeating the same toxic cycles, and passing along the same generational curses. Bouncing back isn't about pretending like the hurt never happened, it's about taking action to heal from the hurt and returning to your original, healthy posture. To heal, you have to face, accept, and make peace with your past. You'll know that you've made peace with your past when you no longer allow it to sabotage your present and future success.

You can start making peace with your past by finding a safe space to face the experiences that have negatively impacted how you feel about yourself, see the world, or interact with other people. It can seem easier to numb your pain and try to ignore its existence, but it will never go away until you acknowledge and deal with it. Acknowledge how you felt at the time and how what you've been through is affecting you now. Say the words you've never said and get out the feelings you've never expressed. You can write in a journal, speak to someone you trust, and/or schedule a session with a mental health professional. If the weight is too heavy for you to carry alone, never feel ashamed to ask for help.

Release grudges and forgive what can't be undone. If someone wronged you, they can't go back in time and undo what they did, but you can choose to forgive them for it now. You can forgive them with or without an apology because the forgiveness you extend is more for you than it is for them. Forgiveness frees you. It detaches you from feelings of anger, hate, and resentment that weigh you down and hold you back. It allows you to move forward with fresh eyes and a whole heart. As long as you have bitterness in your heart, there will always be a part of you that will remain stuck in the past. You have to fully forgive to really move forward.

One of the most powerful steps you can take to make peace with your past is to find purpose in your pain. One of the main reasons why I spend my days empowering, motivating, supporting, and encouraging other women is because I know what feeling powerless, unmotivated, unsupported, and discouraged feels like. Now that I have done the work to heal from my past pain, I can see more clearly how to use it for my benefit and the benefit of others. Now that I am no longer overcome with bitterness and anger from the past, I can appreciate my journey more. I often find myself expressing gratitude for the trials I've been through because I can see how they brought me to where I am today. I am also appreciative of the thoughtfulness that was put into how I was created because I have been able to withstand and survive situations that had the potential to permanently break me. I don't look anything like what I've been through and for that I am extremely grateful.

Two of the biggest barriers to success are a pessimistic mindset and a lack of confidence. Trauma and disappointing experiences can make your world smaller and lonelier, and distort the way you see opportunities and possibilities. To win big, you have to believe in yourself and life's limitless possibilities. You can't be skeptical of everyone and everything. You can't be afraid to step out of your comfort zone. You must have the courage to get back in the ring and keep fighting for your dreams. Do the necessary work to make peace with your past so that you can get out of your own way and rise to your next level.

TAKE A MOMENT.

1. Reflect on the past experiences that have shaped the woman you are today.
2. Are there any experiences that have negatively impacted the way you think, behave, and interact with others? If so, write down what they are.
3. Are you holding any grudges? If so, write down the ways unforgiveness is affecting your life.
4. Who or what is something you need to forgive?

5. Reflect on how you can find purpose in your pain and change the narrative of your story.

6. Is this pain something you can overcome on your own or do you need help? If you need help, reach out to someone you trust and/or mental health professionals in your area.

I am unburdened by the past. I am at peace with where I've been, where I am now, and where I am going. I am releasing all pain and anger that is keeping me from elevating. I am forgiving and forgiven. I am whole, healed, and free.

NOTES

III:

SHE PRIORITIZES HER HEALTH

*She wins because she takes good
care of the vessel she lives in.*

THERE IS NOTHING more important than your health. Not work, not money, not your relationships. If you get sick, you better believe that your employer will find a way to get the job done without you. You can't make money if your mind and body are out of commission. And you can't be fully present for and take care of the people who depend on you if you are not well. I'm going to say it again, you need you to win.

Before I understood this, I burnt myself out on more than one occasion. I neglected my health while working on my goals and trying to please everyone around me. At the time, I thought that putting myself last on my to-do list was a sacrifice worth making and something I should be proud of. I started my days opening my email, posting on social media, and being of service to others instead of praying, exercising, and pouring into myself. I ate what was quick instead of what was healthy. I rested when I could fit it in my schedule, not when my body told me that I needed to. And I eventually paid a heavy price for all of it.

The damage I was doing to myself was not immediately obvious until one day it became blatantly clear that I had been neglecting myself. I woke up one morning, looked in the mirror, and could not recognize the woman staring back at me. It seemed like I gained twenty pounds and aged ten years overnight. I was moving slower and aching in areas I never had ached before. I didn't feel like myself anymore and even my doctors began to show concern for the direction my health was going in. I was financially stable, but physically, emotionally, and spiritually bankrupt. I no longer had the energy to run my business, the motivation to create new products and services, or the ambition to network and engage with other people. I was still young, but so tired. My cup was completely empty and I had nothing left to give. If I wanted to keep going, my only choice was to pause and refill.

"You can't pour from an empty cup." You've likely heard that saying at least once in your life, but are you taking heed to it? You really can't give what you don't have. Much like a car, you can only go so far before you'll have to stop and refuel. That's why it's so important to put yourself at the top of your to-do list. The better you feel, the better your performance will be in all areas of your life. Make it a habit to pour into yourself first so that you will have the energy you need to consistently conquer your days.

Today, prioritizing my self-care is non-negotiable. Before I make myself available to other people, I check in with myself. As the founder of She Wins Society, a Certified Master Life Coach, and motivational speaker, nothing is more important than my mental, physical, emotional, and spiritual health because I lead, guide, and empower other people for a living. I can't do my job effectively and operate in my purpose fully if my energy, focus, confidence, and connection to my Creator are lacking. My mornings now consist of prayer, journaling, yoga, and exercise before I open my email, log into social media, and start accepting others' requests. I schedule regular breaks and take at least two days off each week. I also monitor my water intake and make conscious choices about what I put into my body. Since making these changes, I have not only avoided burnout and regained energy, passion, and ambition, I have also become more productive and profitable.

Your health is your most important asset. You only get one body in this lifetime. Unlike a house, you can't just get up and move when things start falling apart. You have to live with whatever damage you do to yourself, and some damages are irreparable. If you want to win, you have to take care of yourself and prioritize your health. You must be mindful of the foods you consume and the amount of exercise you get. An investment in your health is an investment in your future. There may be seasons when you feel like you can't afford to eat healthily or don't feel like working out, but the truth is that you can't afford not to. If you neglect yourself, it will eventually catch up to you. How you treat yourself today will make a huge difference in how you look and feel years from now. How well you take care of yourself is a major determining factor of how far you'll be able to go and how big you'll be able to win. It's your health over everything.

TAKE A MOMENT.

1. Think about what your best self looks and feels like.
2. Reflect on your current habits as it relates to your physical and mental health. Do your current habits align with the vision you have for your best self?
3. Write down the habits you need to eliminate and implement to feel healthier in the skin you're in.

I am healthy, happy, and hydrated.
I am well-rested and energetic.
I am in the best shape mentally,
physically, and emotionally. I
am thinking clearly and moving
freely. I am fully capable of doing
whatever I set my mind to.

NOTES

IV:

SHE MANAGES HER TIME

*She wins because she creates and commands
her schedule in a way that allows her
to succeed at the highest levels.*

DO YOU REALLY not have enough time or are you wasting too much of the time you have? If you truly want to get the most out of life and reach all of your goals, this is a question you need to answer honestly. I came across a meme on social media that said, "We all have the same 24 hours." At first glance, it seemed accurate, but when I really thought about it, I didn't agree at all. The truth is that a woman with children does not have the same 24 hours as I do. I have several nieces and nephews and friends with children so I know how different time looks when you are responsible for little people. To successfully manage your time, you can't expect your days to look like someone else's. You have to take a look at your own responsibilities and goals and manage your time in a way that works best for you. That means that you may not be able to spend as much time scrolling social media as someone else does. That may also mean that you need to recruit more help. Depending on where you are and the goals you have, you may need to sacrifice more of your leisure time or delegate more of the tasks on your plate to get the most accomplished each day.

As I mentioned in a previous chapter, self-care is non-negotiable and needs to be part of your daily schedule. Putting in the necessary hours to earn a living and spending quality time with your loved ones is also mandatory. Anything that's not adding to your health, happiness, or success is optional. This is the importance of knowing how to say no, both to others and to yourself. If it doesn't align, you probably should decline. This means if it's not in alignment with your goals or the woman you're striving to become, you probably have no business participating in it. You can't be in two places or focus on two things at once, so it's also important to be aware of what you're sacrificing when you choose to go somewhere or give something your attention. One thing you can guarantee about time is that it's going to pass no matter how you choose to spend it. What's questionable is if you will look back at the time you spent with satisfaction or regret.

Once you begin to value your time in a way that makes you think carefully about how you manage it, you will find that you have a lot more time for the things you need to do and the things you want to do. You will stop being busy just for the sake of being busy and you'll also never be bored again. You will increase your productivity levels and accomplish a lot more in short periods of time. You will command your days instead of letting your days command you.

To successfully manage your time, you need to set intentions and boundaries. Before you start each day, evaluate your current goals and deadlines and prioritize your tasks accordingly. Write down what you aim to accomplish each day and hold yourself accountable for sticking to the plan. When you need to work without disruption, eliminate the distractions. That may mean setting your phone to "do not disturb," hiring a babysitter, or going somewhere quiet. Time management is more about your mindset than anything else. If you value your time and understand just how finite it is, you'll be more considerate of how you spend it. Take an audit of how you are currently spending your days. If you find that you're participating in time-wasting activities, ask yourself what else you could be doing to improve the quality of your life. Spending the majority of your time investing in your self-improvement and personal development is a major down payment for your future. I've said it before and I'll say it again, the better you get, the bigger you'll win.

TAKE A MOMENT:

1. Take an audit of how you spend your time on a typical day.
2. Make note of time-wasting activities and adjust where and how you're spending your time as needed.
3. Determine if you can delegate some of your tasks to others to free up more time for yourself.

I am showing appreciation for my life by being a good steward of my time. I am prioritizing my schedule based on what's most important in this season. I am honoring myself by creating healthy boundaries and saying no when I need to. I am living my life in a way that best suits me and my reality.

NOTES

IV:

SHE FACES HER FEARS

*She wins because she acknowledges her
fears, but doesn't let them stop her.*

I HAVE NEVER met a person who was ashamed to say that they are afraid of heights, spiders, or closed spaces. Many of us have those fears in common, so they are a lot less taboo to talk about. It's the fears that most people avoid discussing publicly that are the cause for lack of success. Fears like being afraid to ask for help, answering calls from debt collectors, and failing in front of others. It's the fears that we talk least about that are most often the fears that we must face to elevate beyond our current circumstances.

Asking for help was never my strong suit because it required me to be vulnerable. I spent most of my life thinking that I always needed to be strong so I wasn't comfortable exposing my weaknesses to anyone. As a result, I spent many days suffering and struggling in silence. It took me longer than necessary to accomplish several of my goals because instead of admitting that I didn't know what to do and asking someone who did for help, I took extra time trying to figure it out by myself. I wore my DIY (do-it-yourself) badge with pride until I finally got honest with myself. Trying to do it all alone was slowing me down and burning me out. Wanting more for myself than what I currently had, I had no choice but to face my fear of looking weak to get the help that I needed to level up.

After asking for help the first few times, I realized that I had been making it a lot scarier than it actually was. I found that most people were actually eager to help me and didn't judge me at all for needing help. I also learned something new about myself in the process of asking for help. I discovered that what I was most afraid of was not being vulnerable but being rejected. I overcame my fear of rejection after the first time I reached out for help and was declined. Someone told me no and it wasn't anything like the earth-shattering event I envisioned in my mind. My heart didn't stop and the world didn't end. My feelings weren't even hurt because I didn't take the rejection personally. I just accepted the response and started exploring other ways to get the help I needed. I knew that more options were available to me based on the previous favorable responses I received. Asking for help is now like second nature to me. It's how I've been able to connect with some phenomenal people, build a strong support system, and scale my business. In many ways, facing my fears has made me more fearless.

If you have a fear that is stopping you from achieving one or more of your goals, you owe it to yourself to face it. You can't make progress by standing still or continuously running from the things that make you uncomfortable. At some point, you have to choose between the life you have and the life you want. If you aren't satisfied with where you currently are, you can't stay there. You have to face your fears so that you can move forward and achieve greater. Facing the consequences of your past mistakes and thinking about the potential for future failure can be scary, but what's even scarier is constantly avoiding opportunities to improve the quality of your life. If opening past due bills and talking to debt collectors now will lead to having more financial freedom in the future, it's totally worth it. If trying something new and failing at it teaches you a valuable lesson, it's also worth it. Life is for living, learning, and growing and that's impossible to do if you're crippled by fear. Face your fears head-on now. In the end, you will be so proud of yourself for not letting your fears stop you from living better and winning bigger.

TAKE A MOMENT:

1. Think about your goals. Are there any fears that are keeping you from pursuing them? If so, what are they?
2. Ask yourself what pleasure you will feel if you overcome your fears. Ask yourself what pain you will feel if you don't overcome your fears.

3. Take one step towards overcoming your fear and getting closer to your goals today.
4. Celebrate yourself every time you push past your fears to achieve greater.

I am walking in faith. I am committed to reaching my goals and manifesting my visions no matter what it takes. I am proud of myself for overcoming my fears and completing what I start. I am becoming more fearless and accomplished every day.

NOTES

VI:

SHE FINDS HER TRIBE

She wins because she doesn't live her life to be everyone's cup of tea. She lives her life to attract her tribe.

NOT EVERYONE YOU encounter will like or understand you, but there are plenty of people who will appreciate who you are and all that you bring to the table. The goal is not to be liked by everybody, but to be your authentic self so that you can attract your tribe. The people who see you, get you, and love you for you.

I struggled with finding what I defined as "loyal friends" and maintaining friendships with other women for many years. After several failed friendships and negative interactions, I eventually started to think that it was impossible for women to get along after a certain period of time. Inevitably, there'd be some drama or disagreement that would end the relationship indefinitely. This frustrated me because I really desired friendships that would stand the test of time and a group of friends that I could grow old with. Unwilling to completely give up on the possibility of finding my tribe, I started to evaluate my own actions and what I could potentially change. After all, I was the common denominator in all of my failed relationships.

What I discovered is that I wasn't being true to myself or honest with other people about who I really was. In every relationship, I played a role. I was whoever I thought other people wanted me to be because I was afraid that my authentic self wasn't enough. I cut and pasted pieces of my personality to fit in spaces that I didn't belong in. My relationships weren't sustainable because my true self would eventually show up and make it clear that we were incompatible. We didn't actually like the same things or share similar beliefs and values. They weren't actually my people and I didn't really belong there. It turned out that I was a big part of the problem, but I could now see clearly what I needed to do to fix it. The simple solution was to be authentic.

The key to attracting your soul mate, best friends, loyal supporters, and people who see and appreciate the value your presence brings to the world is to be yourself. I know that this is easier said than done in a society that constantly promotes images and ideas that influence you to believe that you'll be more successful if you look, sound, or act like someone else. However, there's no way to successfully attract your tribe as an imposter or watered down version of yourself. Your authenticity is what allows you to end up in spaces and around people that make being who you are exciting and fulfilling. The risk of being yourself and not being accepted by some people is worth the reward of attracting the people who will accept you wholeheartedly.

You can only go so far alone. If you want to win big, you need a strong support system. Your tribe will provide you with the kind of support you can't get anywhere else. They will accept who you are while encouraging you to become the best version of yourself. They will be understanding when you're not at your best and compassionate when life happens. They will be there to clap for your accomplishments and uplift you when you're feeling discouraged. They will communicate with you instead of cutting you off when there's a disagreement. Your tribe is like your extended family. Even though you may not be biologically related, you share a common energetic bond and vibrate on the same frequency. There is an unspoken understanding between you and your tribe that makes the love unconditional and the support reciprocal. Finding your tribe is one of the most rewarding things you will ever do.

TAKE A MOMENT:

1. Write down the characteristics of the kind of people you want to surround yourself with.

2. Evaluate yourself to see if you give off the kind of energy you want to attract.

3. When given the choice to fit in or stand out, choose to be your authentic self.

I am being true to myself and attracting the people who were created for me. I feel understood and accepted by the people in my circle. I am building honest, trustworthy, and dependable relationships. I am in spaces that I can grow in. I am exactly where I am supposed to be with the people I am meant to be with.

NOTES

VII:

SHE PLAYS FAIR

She wins because she takes the long way when the shortcut requires her to compromise her integrity.

THERE'S NO DENYING that the world is full of people who selfishly lie, scam, and tear others down to further their own agendas. There's also no denying that people who lack integrity and empathy typically have stories with unhappy endings. Their short sightedness causes whatever success they gain to be short-lived. Real winners know the importance of playing fair. They don't try to take unethical or illegal shortcuts, and they don't prey on the easily manipulated or less fortunate to get ahead. Winners do what's right even when they don't feel like it and choose to rise by lifting others.

There have been times on my journey when I questioned if good really wins over evil. I have seen and been in the presence of people who were clearly operating unethically, but still somehow elevating quickly. It perplexed me because I couldn't understand how they were being rewarded for being dishonest, destructive, and manipulative. While I was working hard, operating with integrity, and holding fast to my beliefs and values, I watched people who were doing the complete opposite surpass me. At times, it was really discouraging. However, as it's not in my nature to be evil or intentionally hurt other people, I never once considered shifting to the other side.

Since becoming an entrepreneur and being in business for 7 years, I have doubled down on my belief that operating with honesty and integrity is the best policy. I have no doubt that sticking to my beliefs is one of the main reasons why I have been able to experience such longevity. Many of the people who decided to take devious shortcuts weren't so lucky. Although at one point they seemed to be rising above me, I later looked down to see them crashing below me. That's because you can't trick the universe and you can't hide anything from God. You will always get what you give. If you sow good seeds, you will reap a fruitful harvest. If you sow bad seeds, you will end up on barren land. If you want to win beyond just a few seasons, you have to be willing to play the long game and pass numerous tests to do what's right even when it's tempting to do wrong.

Playing fair is doing your best work and trusting that you will receive the opportunities that are meant for you. It's not stepping on or tearing down others in an attempt to reach your goals. Playing fair is celebrating other women when they win. It's not letting feelings of inadequacy keep you from being inspired by and learning from others' success stories. Playing fair is being honest with people about who you are and the value you can add to their lives. It's not pretending to be something you're not to get what you want at the expense of other people's well-being. Playing fair is being a contributing member of society. It's not always having your hand out and looking for what you can get from others. Playing fair is being your authentic self and operating in your divine purpose. It's not imitating others and stealing their ideas. To win, you have to be what you want to receive. If you want to rise high and stay there, you have to play fair.

TAKE A MOMENT:

1. Define what playing fair means to you.
2. What beliefs do you live by that have proven to be true?

I am operating with excellence and integrity in everything that I do. I am sowing positive seeds and reaping fruitful harvests. I have a great reputation in my family and community. I am creating an inspiring legacy and building a sustainable empire.

NOTES

VIII:

SHE MANIFESTS

She wins because she doesn't just hope and pray,
she also aligns and affirms herself daily.

DON'T UNDERESTIMATE THE power of a pen and paper. If you've been sleeping on positive affirmations, it's time to wake up and win. Positive affirmations are life-changing. Writing and speaking about what you want to see happen in your life is highly effective. There are so many things in my life that have manifested simply because I wrote down that they would. I didn't have to work really hard or jump through a bunch of hoops, I just needed to be paying attention when opportunities presented themselves.

The words you speak are shaping your reality, which is why it's so important to be mindful of what you say. It's not magic, it's energy and intention. Where your mind goes, your body follows. What you focus on grows. If you tell yourself that you can and you really believe it, then you will. If you think about it, that's the start of achieving any goal. Whether it's a weight loss goal, a financial goal, or anything else, achieving it begins with the belief that it's possible for you and the commitment to see it through. Belief is more than half the battle to win.

Journaling positive affirmations are part of my daily morning routine because it gets me in the mindset to win. Before I begin my day, I envision how I want it to go and remind myself of what I'm working towards. Getting in the habit of thinking and speaking positive things about myself also helps me to stay positive throughout the day. Doing so consistently has helped me to train my mind to combat negative thoughts more effectively. I'm much less susceptible to succumb to self-doubt when I experience discouraging situations because I reinforce my self-worth every morning. And I'm much more likely to get what I want because I give off the energy I want to receive daily.

You have the power within you to manifest whatever you want in life. You just have to believe that it's there and tap into it. You tap into it by committing to thinking and speaking only what you want to see and experience. When you catch yourself thinking or speaking in opposition to the life you want to live, immediately swap those thoughts and words with affirmations that are in alignment with who you really want to become. My favorite three words are, "all is well." When I feel myself getting anxious, stressed, or worried, I repeat, "all is well" as many times as needed to avoid going down a rabbit hole of negative thoughts. I don't allow myself to think thoughts that discourage my ambition and that don't serve my well-being. My motto is, "if it doesn't align, I must decline."

Oftentimes, we can be our own toughest critics and meanest bullies, which is why practicing mindfulness and writing positive affirmations is something that I focus on heavily with my coaching clients. I help women to understand the power of their words and change their language to align with their highest good. I teach women how to speak to themselves in a way that builds their confidence and reinforces their self-worth. You can learn more about the personal development and success coaching services I provide at shewinssociety.com.

Mindset and manifestation work together. Once you learn how to master your mind, you'll be in the best position to manifest the grandest life experiences.

TAKE A MOMENT.

1. Remove all limitations from your mind and write down in detail what your best life would look like if you could snap your fingers and live it right now. Include how you look and feel, where you live, what you're doing, and who is around you.
2. Think and speak only what you want to bring into existence from this day forward.
3. Harness positive energy and maintain a positive mindset by writing and saying positive affirmations daily.

I am manifesting the life of my dreams. I am free of mental, physical, and financial limitations. I am living where I want to live and doing work that I love. I am at peace and in alignment with my purpose. My life is unfolding more beautifully than I ever imagined.

NOTES

IX:

SHE WINS

*She wins because she plays the cards that
she's dealt to the best of her ability.*

WINNING ISN'T A specific destination, it's a mindset.
It's a daily decision to believe in yourself, advocate for
yourself, motivate yourself, and bet on yourself. It's having
the determination to get up every time you fall and the
commitment to continue pursuing your goals no matter how
many difficulties, distractions, delays, and disappointments
you experience. Winning is choosing to do the best you
can with what you have every day, and embracing your
journey wholeheartedly.

You don't need to wait until you reach some big goal
that others find worthy of celebration to start feeling like
you've won. You can start feeling like a winner right now by
setting daily goals that give you a sense of satisfaction and

accomplishment. For me, achieving personal goals related to my mental, physical, and emotional health has proved to be much more rewarding than achieving goals meant to prove to others that I am smart, talented, and successful. Plus, having personal goals that are solely based on my actions guarantees that I will be able to celebrate a win every day.

Every day that I wake up and choose to perform activities that benefit my mind, body, and spirit is a cause for celebration. I celebrate myself every morning that I choose to pray, journal, and exercise before I grab my laptop and cell phone. I give myself a big hug every time I make a sacrifice that I know my future self will thank me for. I do a happy dance each time I make a positive impact on someone else's life. I remind myself of my power and ability regularly by looking back on my previous accomplishments. I am very intentional about celebrating both my big and small wins because it's how I stay motivated and make sure that I experience joy and fulfillment daily.

The truth is, if you are putting forth your best effort daily, you are already winning. You are winning because you are learning, growing, improving, and making progress. The only time you lose is when you stop trying and give up on yourself. No one, including me, can tell you what winning should mean to you. However, what I can tell you is that as long as you've clearly defined what winning means to you and you're consciously making choices to live in alignment with that definition, you will experience peace, happiness, and success. Deep down, you already know who you are, what you want, and what you were created to do. If you have the courage to love yourself, be yourself, believe in yourself, honor your needs, create healthy boundaries, embrace change, step out of your comfort zone, walk in your purpose, rise above adversity, and trust the process, you will win.

TAKE A MOMENT:

1. To me, winning means _____.
2. What can you do or change to live more in alignment with your definition of winning?

I am doing the absolute best that I can and it is more than enough. I am showing up as the best version of myself and getting better every day.

NOTES

PART 3

TURN LOSSES INTO WINS

EVERYTHING THAT WE experience in life has a purpose and is meant to move us closer to our divine destiny. Every loss we experience comes with a valuable lesson and a powerful testimony. I believe that our testimonies aren't supposed to be kept a secret because they help to connect us to our tribe and to our calling. They also give us the power to shine light in the darkest times of other people's lives. By sharing our stories, we find more purpose in our own struggles while inspiring others to persevere beyond their own.

Over the years, I have had the pleasure of listening to women from all walks of life share stories both similar to and completely different from mine. What I have found is that no matter where a person comes from or how successful they've become, we all have struggles and we've all experienced losses. I've also found that regardless of how different a woman's story is to mine, there is always something I can relate to and learn from within her perspective.

As I love collaborating with women, and it's very important to me to use my platform to amplify the voices of other women, I invited four members of She Wins Society to join me in sharing true stories of turning losses into wins. The goal is for these stories to inspire you to see that there is life after loss and purpose in your pain. Regardless of where you've been or what you've been through, you can still win. It is my honor to introduce you to Dominique M. Williams, La'Kendrea James, Janet Mingo, and Wilma Blyden.

I:

DOMINIQUE WINS

I HAD JUST relocated to Atlanta, Georgia, and was preparing to celebrate my 24th birthday when I discovered that I was expecting my very first child. To celebrate my birthday, my friend and I went to Las Vegas, and upon returning to Atlanta, my boyfriend flew into town, bought me a Micheal Kors purse, and took me to Pappadeaux restaurant. I had never been and I was eager to eat their food since I'd heard how amazing it was. However, due to pregnancy-induced heartburn, I wasn't able to eat any of my food or enjoy my Spelman College-themed cake that my friend bought me. Nevertheless, I enjoyed my birthday festivities, and took the pregnancy test later that week to confirm what I already suspected.

A short time later, I traveled back to Ohio, my hometown, because I hadn't secured a job as a Registered Nurse in Atlanta yet, and had grown bored. While there, I went and heard the baby's heartbeat, and received my very first ultrasound. At the time, it was like music to my ears, but soon after, I regretted hearing it. I went from enjoying my visit with my family and friends to finding myself grieving the loss of my unborn child that was to be born on May 3, 2013. When I was 10 weeks along, my boyfriend and I went to my first OB appointment in October 2012 to confirm pregnancy. My joy quickly turned to horror as no heartbeat was found. I was crushed, devastated, and defeated. I was told I would need a dilation and curettage (D & C), a procedure to remove the baby from inside my uterus. I couldn't even begin to process the removal of my baby as we were just introduced to one another, but since my body hadn't recognized fetal death, the surgery was imminent so it didn't pose a risk to my health. Hearing this news, I cried and cried until I had a headache and felt physically ill.

The morning of the procedure, I had them perform another ultrasound to confirm that there was no heartbeat as I was still in denial. Unfortunately, the ultrasound confirmed the worst case scenario. I had the procedure and was on the road to recovery, but there was a hole in my heart. I went through all of the stages of grief (denial, anger, bargaining, and depression) except for acceptance at the time. I was in denial that my baby died. I was angry that my baby died, while other babies were being born. While I wanted to be happy for those around me, my own pain was too intense. I began to question God, and everything

I knew up until that point. I didn't understand what I had done to deserve this. I felt so low, and I went even lower when people would make insensitive remarks like, "The Lord giveth and the Lord taketh away," "You can have one of my kids/grandkids," "Do you have children?" "What are you waiting on?"

I was desperately trying to conceive again and on Valentine's Day of 2013, my prayers were answered. I discovered the great news in the month of March. I gave birth to my rainbow baby, a baby girl, on November 13, 2013. To people on the outside looking in, conceiving again happened rapidly, but to me, it seemed like an eternity. Talk about a triumphant win after such a traumatic loss. It was nothing but God that kept me from going insane while waiting for my blessing. I ran to church and prayed more than ever before. I also wrote a poem about my unborn baby after speaking with my pastor who advised me to do so. That was a very therapeutic exercise, especially since I am passionate about expressing myself through writing. While time passing helped, being able to conceive again ultimately helped me cope with the loss. However, I would highly recommend grief counseling to anyone coping with a similar loss.

I now understand that it was all a part of God's divine plan and that without a test, there is no testimony. I am a testament to resilience and perseverance. I possess the strength, determination, and will to overcome anything. God has allowed me to be triumphant over various life experiences which have strengthened my faith muscle. Adversity is a part of life which allows us to fully experience joy. No matter what we may be experiencing, we must remember to give God the glory.

Dominique M. Williams

INSIDE OF ME BY DOMINIQUE M. WILLIAMS

I have a beautiful baby growing inside of me.
Created from the intense passion of two busy bees.
I have a beautiful baby growing inside of me.
Birth date in the spring on day three.
I have a beautiful baby growing inside of me.
That beautiful day I never got to see.
I have a beautiful baby growing inside of me.
No flowers, no showers, and no more mommy to be.
I have a beautiful baby growing inside of me.
For my face was filled with glee until there was no heartbeat visible to see.
I have a beautiful baby growing inside of me.
This pain hurt and agony I couldn't believe.
I had a beautiful baby growing inside of me.

NOTES

II:

LA'KENDREA WINS

I AM LA'KENDREA James; Wife, Mother, Women's Empowerment Blogger, U.S. Air Force Sergeant, and She Wins Society's Motherhood Group Coach. Before I was all of this, I was a girl in love with a boy. I met my ex-husband back in 2010. I was fresh off a four-month tour to Iraq. I had been back in the country for a little over a week when we met through a mutual friend. Before I give you the timeline and details, it is important for you to understand a little about me. I was a young girl on a quest to find love. I was often in and out of relationships hoping and praying that someone would love me past my flaws. When I met my ex-husband, I was vulnerable and open and just wanted to be shown attention and love no matter what that love looked like. I fell in love with his sense of humor and his care for me, but that all quickly changed. The timeline from the day that we officially started dating and got married was extremely short. He moved in within a week, we started entertaining thoughts about getting married, and within two months we were married.

The night before we got married, I felt a pit in my stomach that told me we shouldn't, but I didn't listen. You could tell that the wedding was rushed. We had no family, no real plans, just two people in what seemed like love. After the wedding, everything from two months prior changed. My laughs turned into tears, my joy into pain, even my apartment grew dark. My heart was numb from the emotional and physical pain I had endured at the hands and mouth of the one person who vowed to love me forever. Over the next few months, we had several physical and emotional altercations. Hurtful words spoken were embedded in my mind. Memories of being choked and shoved into walls, doors, and to the ground, having bloody and swollen lips, screaming for help until I was able to fight my way out were created. Abuse comes in cycles, so we would make up for maybe a week or so at a time, and then be right back to square one. I was hurting, ashamed, and very much alone. I could not tell anyone what I was going through as I was not ready to hear, "I told you so." I grew depressed, but I tried to fight it.

Throughout all of this madness, I found out that I was expecting. It was exciting, but I was so nervous because I had never been a mom before and the person I created this child with no longer treated me as his wife or like he even cared at all. In fact, we were not even living in the same house when I found out that I was pregnant because we had a no contact order. We later relocated to Georgia and things were okay for a couple of weeks. I hoped that a new location would bring new behavior moving forward, but the old habits remained. I discovered infidelity within our marriage. Already pregnant, emotional, and feeling unattractive, my depression got worse.

When my son was born, I thought that would make everything okay. I thought that he would want to be home with us and that he would stop treating me like I was just some woman off the street. He treated strangers a lot better than he did me. While I was depressed and raising a baby on my own, yet still married, he was out living his life, not even worrying about how he destroyed me emotionally. Time heals physical wounds, but emotional ones last forever, or at least until you get help. He came back and I let him in one last and final time. The final straw was an altercation that took place in front of my then 1-year-old son. That July night in 2012, I chose me and my son. My son hugged me that night and his embrace even at 1-year old let me know that we were going to be alright. It was time for me to step off the rollercoaster that my life had been over the last couple of years. My road to rebuilding was everything. I finally got the help that I needed by attending therapy sessions. I got back into church and finally got my life on track. My spirits were lifted and the hard life that I had endured for so long was no longer hard. My apartment did not feel dark anymore, my smile got brighter, and I found joy in the simple things in life.

As I continued to work on myself, I divorced my ex-husband (it took over a year) and met my current husband, Andre, during a tour to Korea. We were married in 2015, have four beautiful children, and we just purchased our first home. I am using my story and my trauma to help uplift, empower, restore, and rebuild other women. I started a blog called Every Queen Empowered to share my experiences with other women so that they do not feel alone or ashamed like I did in those dark times. I believe God uses our messes and turns them into messages. My message is that my past does not define me. It no longer has power over me, and I am not a victim of domestic violence. I am a domestic violence survivor!

La'Kendrea James

"You were a warrior from the womb, and your entrance was a victory. From the moment you opened your mouth, they knew you were a prophetess. In your lungs was a war cry. Your hands fit to hold swords, and angels sang. Remember this the next time it feels like the weight of the world is engraved in your spine.
Do not shrink. Rise."
- Yecheilyah Ysrayl

NOTES

III:

JANET WINS

I CAN REMEMBER it just like it was yesterday, being in high school and wanting a miracle to happen. From a young age, I knew I was going to be the one to change the dynamics of my family. I created a five-year plan and I was determined to go to college. Becoming a physical therapist was my dream. It was the road map to eradicate all of my mom's struggles. I just wanted things to get easier, regardless of what that meant for me. I denied my own desires to participate in volleyball, drama, and chorus so that I could pick up extra work hours.

As the middle child of five, I grew up feeling misunderstood. I felt like if I could just make it easier I would have completed my mission. However, growing up with Marfan Syndrome, I already felt as if I was a burden on my family. I actually found my love for physical therapy in middle school. After having to learn how to walk for the 7th time, I was mentally disgusted with myself. There were times when I didn't want to take another step, and I would ask God, "Why?" I would question him during my low moments. I would often ponder the same questions, "God why did I have to get bullied?," and, "God, why couldn't you just make me normal like my brothers and sisters?"

What is normal anyway? It's crazy when you are in the midst of the pain, sometimes we can feel like that is our stopping point.

From the moment I was of age to work, I became a workaholic. I picked up one job and I maintained two positions before graduating high school. Little did I know, I was creating the foundation to have the "superwoman" mentality. I adopted this mentality too early in life. When I was tired or wanted to call out, I couldn't. I would remind myself of how I didn't want my nephew Miyazaki to wake up and say, "My auntie Janet failed me!" So I never gave myself a free day, and I just kept moving on fumes. By the time I made it to college, I still had the same work ethic. I don't even know why I lived on campus honestly. I was at work more than I was on campus. During my first semester, I took 19 credit hours and I don't know how I maintained a 3.7 GPA. However, by the time my junior year came around, I was mentally and physically exhausted. I had been carrying everyone's burdens and never took the time to care for myself. I was everyone's "superwoman." For instance, one night someone woke me after a double shift. This individual knew my schedule, and asked me for a ride. I told them that my gas tank was on E, and this person's response was, "I only need a ride up the street, and God will bless you." It was at that moment I realized I could not keep on the way that I was going. I had to stop overexerting myself for others and start filling my own cup.

Quick Question: How many rides have you given that stunted your growth? How many distractions have come your way when you are trying to do something for yourself? Heck, almost every time I started to write this paragraph someone wanted to call me.

I knew I needed freedom. I knew I wanted my nephews, nieces, and godchildren to see the difference that I made. I wanted them to wake up without uncontrollable hurt. I wanted them to be genuinely happy! I wanted them not to feel like they had to choose a part-time job over their high school sport or passion. I yearned to make an impact, but I was also tired. I was tired of feeling stagnant. I was tired of having the exact same new year's resolution for five years in a row.

I knew something needed to change and I had to be responsible for that change. I wanted to show up for myself, just like I had when I woke up for someone else at 3 o'clock in the morning, and not feel guilty. I was a great employee, a great colleague, and the great friend everyone could count on, but for so long my own desires were buried. I was so used to showing up for others, but showing up for myself felt foreign. One night, I finally invested in myself by joining "She Wins Society," formerly known as "Women By Choice". This was a complete breath of fresh air. While on the road to Atlanta for an Authors Book Camp hosted by one of our sisters, I declared that it was time for me to give it my all. I decided I was going to stop putting my dreams on the back burner. I decided to stop pouring from an empty cup. I decided to focus on my brand, and to stop pretending that I was working behind the scenes. I was so sick and tired of waking up each and every day and not having any of my personal dreams accomplished. No one knew I had these feelings because of my accolades, titles, and accomplishments. I had all of those tangible things, but I felt empty because I wasn't doing anything for myself. I wasn't creating the lifestyle that I wanted to live. Honestly, I was far from happy and couldn't even paint a vivid picture of how happiness looked. After I had this huge "come to Jesus" moment, a couple of hours later, I was rear-ended in my car. I could not believe it. I was traveling from Suffolk, Virginia to Atlanta, Georgia to change; being rear-ended was not on my agenda.

The accident occurred in Spartanburg, South Carolina, which was my halfway mark. I was rear-ended by a young driver who literally had just earned her license and was on her way to a job interview. At that moment, I didn't know what to expect. I was scared, in a rental car, and on top of that, my mother was just in a car accident that severely damaged her spine. I was praying, "Please let everything be okay, I have to be there for my mom!" I was at my breaking point. I couldn't take one more thing or ounce of negativity. I was so drained and tired of setbacks, but I needed to keep going. I couldn't wait to get to the event, and be in the atmosphere of the boot camp. I needed to be around people who understood that their goals were achievable. I needed to be around visionaries who had a good work ethic. So I kept driving to Georgia, although a part of me wanted to turn right around and go back home. I kept driving as one of my best friends was trying to encourage me, but I didn't want to hear it, I just wanted to get out of the car.

After a sincere look in the mirror, I decided that just showing up wasn't enough for me anymore. I decided that I wouldn't let that setback stop me. I was going to show up to the event, and I was going to give my brand my all. In order to do that, I had to get realistic about my expectations and the changes that I had to make. I had to really think about what steps I was willing to take to achieve what I wanted. That night I couldn't sleep. I was thinking and two quotes came to mind. Who knew those two quotes would turn out to become my best-selling products? On a whim, I placed an order of 62 shirts with each quote. With no experience, I launched my website and had my best friend take my branding photos. Within a week, I sold out of my first order of inventory. I had no clue where to start, I just knew that I had to! It was seriously my time. After truly realizing that I was enough, I addressed all of the hidden insecurities and let them go. I knew that if God made that happen, He would continue to show up and allow me to win again. I just had to trust the process!

Sis, you can win again! As I type the words on this page, I want to encourage you. The pain isn't where the experience stops. It was actually during my pain and feeling misunderstood, that I grew a heart for people. Then after the struggle, I realized I wasn't created to heal bones, but to heal hearts. You were made for your dreams! You were created to not only shift the atmosphere but to make an impact! I believe in you!

Janet Mingo

Today, I commit to listening to my body and honoring my needs. I am worthy of my time and attention.
- Dr. Robyn Gobin

NOTES

IV:

WILMA WINS

I WAS TAUGHT the Church is not a building, it's the people who make up the Church. After my car accident, I knew I would stop attending Church for a short period. The car accident was a short distance from the church building, and I stood in disbelief as I looked towards the direction of the church building and saw some members of the Church standing in the churchyard looking on from a distance.

The Good Samaritan story in Luke 10 came to mind when the Usher was the only person from the Church that came to the scene of the accident. The Usher was shocked when noticing that I was involved in a vehicular accident and asked if I was okay. I often wondered what the Church's members' reasons were for not visiting the scene to determine if the drivers were okay. The accident caused the traffic to be blocked Eastbound and Westbound for 45 minutes while waiting for the police to arrive.

I was disappointed and felt abandoned by the Church. I expected the Church to be there, I expected the Church to show compassion, I expected love from the Church. Through journaling, I expressed my feelings, and it helped me release my expectations of the Church, but before releasing the expectations, I had to figure out why I had those expectations in the first place.

I'd been attending that Church and was taught Christianity is what is done, not what is said. When I reflected on the Church's attributes on the day of the accident, the scripture in James 1:22 came to mind, "But be ye doers of the word, and not hearers only, deceiving yourselves." I wanted to be a part of a church that was moved by compassion and a church that desired to be Christlike in Word and in deed.

I contacted a few church members and asked their reasons for not visiting the accident scene or contacting me to determine if I was okay. Their responses were, "I didn't want to be in your business," "I heard you were not hurt," "I had to go to a birthday party for my niece," "you give off a facial expression and an aura that you don't want people to be around you," "I didn't know." The accident happened in July 2020, and I haven't visited the Church since. After hearing those responses and receiving no contact from the ministerial and leadership, I left the Church.

This was a difficult decision to make and a significant step to take. I was on an untrodden path. I felt my decision to leave the Church was wrong because scripture states not to forsake the gathering of brethren together. I believe that I am a tripartite being spirit, body, and soul, and I wanted to be part of a church that cared for my spiritual, physical, and emotional wellbeing. I've seen men and women die, believing in things that never came to pass, and always wondered why they didn't change their strategy. If they were operating a business and were making a loss at the end of every year, they would surely change the business strategy. I needed to change my strategy as it related to the Church.

After leaving the Church, I started to spend uninterrupted time with God. I expressed in my journal to Him that I felt abandoned by the Church and that I wanted to know Him. One of the scriptures I spent a lot of time reading and studying was Psalms 23.

Most people view restoration as being restored to who they were before pain, challenges, or disappointment occurred in their life. Through revelation, I understand restoration is to be restored to God's original plan and purpose for your life. When God restores you, He leads you on the path of righteousness. If God is leading you, He is walking in front of you. God will lead you to show you how to live a righteous life. The scripture tells us in Psalms 23, "Yea though you walk through the valley of death, you will fear no evil because God is with you." During the restoration, the past will resurface, but you must remember that your past is behind you. It's just a shadow, you must keep walking forward because God is with you. Being restored will only be unfamiliar to you if you are unsure of God's plan and purpose for your life. To avoid uncertainty, ask God what His plans and purpose are for your life. After all, He created you, and He knows you better than you know yourself.

After spending time in God's presence, I began to view the car accident as a trial and see that God was allowing the enemy to test my ability to forgive. But how could I forgive the Church? The Church that didn't check in on me after the accident. The Church that I stopped attending, and still, no one checked on me. How could I forgive the Church that has not asked for forgiveness? Isn't it true, if someone doesn't ask for forgiveness, it's because they don't think they have done anything wrong? How could I forgive the Church?

God led me to 1 John 4:7, which states, "Beloved, let us love one another: for love is of God, and every one that loveth is born of God and knoweth God." While spending uninterrupted time in God's presence, I learned attributes of my biblical identity. The first characteristic of the fruits of the Spirit is LOVE. God is love. There is no way you can spend time in His presence and not have love. What helped me forgive the Church was LOVE.

The other scriptures that God lead me to were:

1 Corinthians 13:2, "If I have the gift of prophecy and can fathom all mysteries and all knowledge, and if I have a faith that can move mountains, but do not have love, I am nothing."

1 Corinthians 13:13, "And now these three remain, faith, hope, and love. But the greatest of these is love."

Romans 13:8, "Owe no man anything, but to love one another: for he that loveth another hath fulfilled the law."

To turn trials into triumph, my encouragement to you is:

(1) Love. 1 Peter 4:8, "Above all, love each other deeply because love covers a multitude of sins."

(2) Spend uninterrupted time in God's presence; He will teach you how to turn trials into triumphs.

There is a quote by Gandhi, "Be the change that you want to see in the world." If I want love from the Church, I have to show love to the Church. I wrote a letter to the Church forgiving the Church and returned to Church and created the change that I wanted. We are tripartite beings. We ought to love each other spiritually, physically, and emotionally.

The Bible shares in 1 Corinthians 13:4-8 sixteen characteristics of LOVE, "Love is patient, love is kind. It does not envy, it does not boast, it is not proud. It does not dishonor others, it is not self-seeking, it is not easily angered, it keeps no record of wrongs. Love does not delight in evil but rejoices with the truth. It always protects, always trusts, always hopes, always perseveres. Love never fails."

Wilma Blyden

Sis, sometimes you gotta pray for understanding to understand.
- Nikki Gillis

NOTES

V:

ANDROMEDA WINS

WHEN I GOT the call that my godmother was being rushed to the hospital, I never fathomed that I would hear the news I received shortly after. Although she was in her 70's, and I sometimes had fleeting thoughts that her life was getting shorter, losing her anytime soon was the furthest thing from my mind. She was a vegetarian, active most of her life, kind to others, and made many sacrifices for the ones she loved, so I always saw her as someone who deserved to live a joyful life and experience a painless death. When my mother called to give me an update on my godmother's diagnosis, I was in shock and instantly heartbroken. I'm sure much more was said, but all that I heard was, "It's stage 4 cancer. There's nothing the doctors can do. She has less than 6 months to live." Remembering her as a marathon runner who practiced karate and overcame so much adversity throughout her lifetime, I didn't want to believe that she couldn't overcome this too. I told myself that she was a fighter and that for all the good she has done for others, God will save her. She passed away less than 3 weeks later.

You might be wondering how I could find any wins in such a traumatic loss, but one thing I know for sure is that my godmother would want me to find purpose in my pain. She lived her life trusting God through all things and in her last days, she made peace with her fate. Even as she laid in a hospital bed knowing her life was coming to an end, she still expressed love for God and love for me. In the last conversation we had, she laughed and encouraged me to not waste time worrying about frivolous things. She reminded me that in the end, what will matter most is not the degrees, monetary gains, and accolades, but the love you gave and the impact you made. I will forever be changed by her life and her death.

Losing my godmother gave me a new sense of what's most important in life. It made me slow down and appreciate every moment. It made me stop taking the people I love for granted. It made me live in a more meaningful and purposeful way. The way she departed also inspired me to stop neglecting my health and address the issues I was having with my doctors. She had been suffering with cancer long before her final hospital visit, but she never went to the doctor to address her symptoms. This was a huge wake-up call for me to prioritize my health and it inspired me to encourage other women not to wait to seek help only when they see changes in their bodies. I know that she would be happy that I'm using her story to serve others because serving is what she delighted in.

Aneesah was one of the most amazing women I have ever known. Although she was small in stature, she was strong in heart. She was tiny but mighty. She was unapologetic about her faith and lived fully in her truth. She wasn't ashamed to be who she was and she didn't hide her flaws or dim her light to make others comfortable. She kept her word and gave her absolute best to everything that she did. When she smiled, she meant it. And when she was upset, you knew it. She wasn't afraid to try new experiences and learn new things. She was always up for a challenge and finished what she started. She learned how to speak Arabic and bake bread from scratch. She completed multiple marathons, earned a brown belt in karate, and earned a degree in education. She valued family, adored teaching children, and truly loved unconditionally. She would give her last to someone in need and was always grateful for the little things.

Unfortunately, we can't always see how great something is until it's gone. Losing my godmother helped me to see the impact her life made on mine more clearly and tap deeper into the greatness within me so that I can continue her legacy of love, integrity, faith, perseverance, and authenticity. Because she lived so fully and fearlessly, I can win bigger than the generations that came before me.

Andromeda Raheem

"Sometimes you will feel like you're soaring above the clouds and sometimes you will feel like you're crashing to the ground. Experiencing highs and lows in life is normal. Choosing to move with grace, faith, and gratitude through all situations and circumstances is how you continuously grow and win."
- Andromeda Raheem

NOTES

ABOUT THE AUTHOR

ANDROMEDA RAHEEM IS a Certified Master Life Coach, the founder of She Wins Society, and author of *She Wins: The Ultimate Guide for Women to Gain a Winning Mindset and Lead a Winning Lifestyle*. For nearly a decade, Andromeda has worked to empower women to be confident in their authentic selves, overcome limiting beliefs, and manifest the lives they truly desire and deserve. Even before she began coaching women professionally, Andromeda has always been passionate about motivating women to do their best and manifest their dreams. She has been recognized for her efforts to unite and empower women by Ambassadors of Change Inc. and featured in several reputable publications including The Huffington Post, Sheen Magazine, and Rolling Out. Andromeda's ability to effectively communicate with women in a way that engages their attention and uplifts their spirits has also garnered worldwide recognition on social media and an Instagram following of over 100,000.

Andromeda currently resides in Orlando, Florida with her husband. To learn more about She Wins Society's membership community and Andromeda's coaching programs and self-care retreats, please visit shewinssociety.com.

CONNECT WITH THE AUTHOR

Website: shewinssociety.com
Instagram: @shewinssociety
Facebook: She Wins Society